Watch Out, Charlie Brown

Selected cartoons from
"YOU'RE OUT OF SIGHT,
CHARLIE BROWN, VOLUME 2"

Charles M. Schulz

CORONET BOOKS
Hodder Fawcett, London

Copyright © 1970 by United Feature Syndicate, Inc.

First published 1975 by Fawcett Publications, Inc.,
New York

Coronet edition 1977
Second impression 1978

Printed in Great Britain for Hodder
Fawcett Ltd., Mill Road, Dunton Green,
Sevenoaks, Kent (Editorial Office:
47 Bedford Square, London, WC1 3DP) by
C. Nicholls & Company Ltd
The Philips Park Press, Manchester

ISBN 0 340 21797 9

TELL ME THAT YOU LOVE ME, KISS ME ON THE NOSE AND GIVE ME A BIG HUG!

LOOK OUT, EVERYBODY! I'M GONNA BE CRABBY FOR THE REST OF THE DAY!!

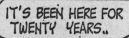

3. How many owls did you howl at?
"TWELVE, BUT I SAW ONLY TWO"...STUPID OWLS!
4. Did you take part in any Fox Hunts?
"NO"... I HAVE NO DESIRE TO BE
STOMPED ON BY A CLUMSY HORSE!

THIS IS THE PART I HATE...
5. Relationships with humans....
    a. How did you treat your master?
    b. Were you friendly with neighborhood children?
    c. Did you bite anyone?
THESE ARE VERY PERSONAL QUESTIONS...

Return the yellow form to the Head Beagle with your dues, and keep the blue form for your files..Report must be postmarked no later than Jan. 15th

WHAT A NUISANCE..

I'D REALLY LIKE TO JUST FORGET THE WHOLE THING..

U.S. MAIL

EXCEPT THAT SOMEDAY I MAY GET TO BE THE HEAD BEAGLE!

➤➤➤

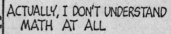

BOY, DID YOU EVER GOOF ME UP!

YOU HAD ME TAKE MY LUNCH TO SCHOOL IN A LUNCH BOX... DO YOU KNOW WHAT HAPPENED?

ALL THE OTHER KIDS WERE BROWN-BAGGING IT!! I FELT LIKE A FOOL!

YOU GAVE ME BAD ADVICE, BIG BROTHER!

I CAN'T STAND ALL THIS RESPONSIBILITY..

BOOT!

I LOST YOUR FOOTBALL, BIG BROTHER...I KICKED IT SO HIGH IT NEVER CAME DOWN..

DON'T WORRY ABOUT IT... IT'LL COME DOWN...

BIG BROTHERS KNOW EVERYTHING!

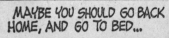

HOW DO YOU TELL A PUMPKIN THAT YOU DON'T NEED HIM ANY MORE?

THE HOME TEAM WAS BEHIND SIX-TO-NOTHING WITH ONLY THREE SECONDS TO PLAY..THEY HAD THE BALL ON THEIR OWN ONE-YARD LINE...

THE QUARTERBACK TOOK THE BALL, FADED BACK BEHIND HIS OWN GOAL POSTS AND THREW A PERFECT PASS TO THE LEFT END, WHO WHIRLED AWAY FROM FOUR GUYS AND RAN ALL THE WAY FOR A TOUCHDOWN! THE FANS WENT WILD! YOU SHOULD HAVE SEEN THEM!

PEOPLE WERE JUMPING UP AND DOWN, AND WHEN THEY KICKED THE EXTRA POINT, THOUSANDS OF PEOPLE RAN OUT ONTO THE FIELD LAUGHING AND SCREAMING! THE FANS AND THE PLAYERS WERE SO HAPPY THEY WERE ROLLING ON THE GROUND AND HUGGING EACH OTHER AND DANCING AND EVERYTHING!

IT WAS FANTASTIC!

HOW DID THE OTHER TEAM FEEL?

FORTY-ONE!
SEVEN!
FIFTEEN!

MY CENTER HAS DIFFICULTY
GETTING THE BALL BACK...

HI, CHUCK... SORRY YOU MISSED THE GAME YESTERDAY...

I SURE HAVE TO HAND IT TO YOU, THOUGH, CHUCK... THAT WAS SOME TEAM YOU SENT OVER... THEY CLOBBERED US, BUT GOOD!

TEAM?

THAT FUNNY LOOKING KID WITH THE BIG NOSE WAS GREAT, AND THOSE LITTLE GUYS HE HAD WITH HIM WERE ALL OVER THE FIELD!

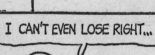

HERE I AM PRACTICING FOR THE WORLD FIGURE-SKATING CHAMPIONSHIP IN YUGOSLAVIA..

I'LL PROBABLY CATCH A FLIGHT OUT OF NEW YORK ON FEBRUARY TWENTY-SEVENTH...

I'LL ARRIVE IN ZURICH IN THE MORNING, AND CONNECT WITH ANOTHER FLIGHT TO ZAGREB...

THIS IS GOING TO BE A BAD CHRISTMAS..

ALL MY LETTERS TO SANTA CLAUS CAME BACK UNOPENED!

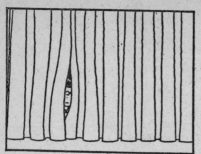

"THE ANNUAL SPORTS BANQUET HELD HERE LAST NIGHT WAS A HUGE SUCCESS."

"SPORTS CELEBRITIES FROM ALL OVER THE NATION ATTENDED..THE ONLY ATHLETE MISSING WAS BASEBALL PLAYER JOE SHLABOTNIK."

"JOE APOLOGIZED TO REPORTERS THIS MORNING..HE EXPLAINED THAT HE HAD MARKED THE WRONG DATE ON HIS CALENDAR, THE WRONG CITY AND THE WRONG EVENT..."

HE'S *YOUR* HERO, CHARLIE BROWN!

SIGH

FOR THE LOVE OF PEANUTS

All these books are available at your local bookshop or newsagent, or can be ordered direct from the publisher. Just tick the titles you want and fill in the form below.
Prices and availability subject to change without notice.

CORONET BOOKS, P.O. Box 11, Falmouth, Cornwall.
Please send cheque or postal order, and allow the following for postage and packing:
U.K. – One book 22p plus 10p per copy for each additional book ordered, up to a maximum of 82p.
B.F.P.O. and EIRE – 22p for the first book plus 10p per copy for the next 6 books, thereafter 4p per book.
OTHER OVERSEAS CUSTOMERS – 30p for the first book and 10p per copy for each additional book.

Name...

Address...

....